FRANCIS FRITH'S

OAKHAM PHOTOGRAPHIC MEMORIES

THE FRANCIS FRITH COLLECTION

www.francisfrith.com

FRANCIS FRITH'S

OAKHAM

PHOTOGRAPHIC MEMORIES

BRYAN WAITES has lived in Oakham for over 30 years. He was a founder member of the Rutland Record Society and for 12 years its first editor. He was elected Honorary Life Member for his services to the Society and to the history of Rutland. He was a teacher at Oakham School, and previously at Leicester Polytechnic and the University of Loughborough. He is a graduate in History and Geography of the University of Keele and the Institute of Historical Research. His recent publications include *Monasteries and Landscape in North-East England, Walks in Historic Leicestershire and Rutland, Pub Strolls in Leicestershire and Rutland* and many other books on walking.

FRANCIS FRITH'S
PHOTOGRAPHIC MEMORIES

OAKHAM

PHOTOGRAPHIC MEMORIES

BRYAN WAITES

First published in the United Kingdom in 2003 by
Frith Book Company Ltd

Limited Hardback Subscribers Edition Published in 2003
ISBN 1-85937-797-1

Paperback Edition 2003
ISBN 1-85937-612-6

British Library Cataloguing in Publication Data

Francis Frith's Oakham - Photographic Memories
Bryan Waites
ISBN 1-85937-612-6

Frith Book Company Ltd
Frith's Barn, Teffont,
Salisbury, Wiltshire SP3 5QP
Tel: +44 (0) 1722 716 376
Email: info@francisfrith.co.uk
www.francisfrith.co.uk

Printed and bound in Great Britain

Front Cover: **OAKHAM,** *Market Place 1932* 85151c
Frontispiece: **OAKHAM,** *Old Buttercross and Stocks 1927* 80280

Acknowledgements
The author and publishers are grateful to the following for
their help: Margot Fitzpatrick, George Kirk, Kathleen Lovett,
Alison Parkhouse, J D Proudman, Betty Tidd, A R Traylen,
Ken Weatherhogg.

*The colour-tinting is for illustrative purposes only, and is not intended to be
historically accurate*

AS WITH ANY HISTORICAL DATABASE THE FRITH ARCHIVE IS CON-
STANTLY BEING CORRECTED AND IMPROVED AND THE PUBLISHERS
WOULD
WELCOME INFORMATION ON OMISSIONS OR INACCURACIES

CONTENTS

FRANCIS FRITH
VICTORIAN PIONEER

FRANCIS FRITH, founder of the world-famous photographic archive, was a complex and multi-talented man. A devout Quaker and a highly successful Victorian businessman, he was philosophic by nature and pioneering in outlook.

By 1855 he had already established a wholesale grocery business in Liverpool, and sold it for the astonishing sum of £200,000, which is the equivalent today of over £15,000,000. Now a very rich man, he was able to indulge his passion for travel. As a child he had pored over travel books written by early explorers, and his fancy and imagination had been stirred by family holidays to the sublime mountain regions of Wales and Scotland. 'What lands of spirit-stirring and enriching scenes and places!' he had written. He was to return to these scenes of grandeur in later years to 'recapture the thousands of vivid and tender memories', but with a different purpose. Now in his thirties, and captivated by the new science of photography, Frith set out on a series of pioneering journeys up the Nile and to the Near East that occupied him from 1856 until 1860.

INTRIGUE AND EXPLORATION

These far-flung journeys were packed with intrigue and adventure. In his life story, written when he was sixty-three, Frith tells of being held captive by bandits, and of fighting 'an awful midnight battle to the very point of surrender with a deadly pack of hungry, wild dogs'. Wearing flowing Arab costume, Frith arrived at Akaba by camel seventy years before Lawrence of Arabia, where he encountered 'desert princes and rival sheikhs, blazing with jewel-hilted swords'.

He was the first photographer to venture beyond the sixth cataract of the Nile. Africa was still the mysterious 'Dark Continent', and Stanley and Livingstone's historic meeting was a decade into the future. The conditions for picture taking confound belief. He laboured for hours in his wicker dark-room in the sweltering heat of the desert, while the volatile chemicals fizzed dangerously in their trays. Back in London he exhibited his photographs and was 'rapturously cheered' by members of the Royal Society. His reputation as a photographer was made overnight.

VENTURE OF A LIFE-TIME

Characteristically, Frith quickly spotted the opportunity to create a new business as a specialist publisher of photographs. He lived in an era of immense and sometimes violent change.

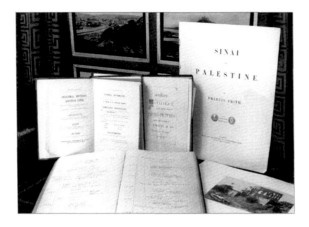

For the poor in the early part of Victoria's reign work was exhausting and the hours long, and people had precious little free time to enjoy themselves. Most had no transport other than a cart or gig at their disposal, and rarely travelled far beyond the boundaries of their own town or village. However, by the 1870s the railways had threaded their way across the country, and Bank Holidays and half-day Saturdays had been made obligatory by Act of Parliament. All of a sudden the working man and his family were able to enjoy days out and see a little more of the world.

With typical business acumen, Francis Frith foresaw that these new tourists would enjoy having souvenirs to commemorate their days out. In 1860 he married Mary Ann Rosling and set out on a new career: his aim was to photograph every city, town and village in Britain. For the next thirty years he travelled the country by train and by pony and trap, producing fine photographs of seaside resorts and beauty spots that were keenly bought by millions of Victorians. These prints were painstakingly pasted into family albums and pored over during the dark nights of winter, rekindling precious memories of summer excursions.

THE RISE OF FRITH & CO

Frith's studio was soon supplying retail shops all over the country. To meet the demand he gathered about him a small team of photographers, and published the work of independent artist-photographers of the calibre of Roger Fenton and Francis Bedford. In order to gain some understanding of the scale of Frith's business one only has to look at the catalogue issued by Frith & Co in 1886: it runs to some 670 pages, listing not only many thousands of views of the British Isles but also many photographs of most European countries, and China, Japan, the USA and Canada - note the sample page shown here from the hand-written Frith & Co ledgers recording the pictures. By 1890 Frith had created the greatest specialist photographic publishing company in the world, with over 2,000 sales outlets - more than the combined number that Boots and WH Smith have today! The picture on the next page shows the Frith & Co display board at Ingleton in the Yorkshire Dales (left of window). Beautifully constructed with a mahogany frame and gilt inserts, it could display up to a dozen local scenes.

POSTCARD BONANZA

The ever-popular holiday postcard we know today took many years to develop. In 1870 the Post Office issued the first plain cards, with a pre-printed stamp on one face. In 1894 they allowed other publishers' cards to be sent through the mail with an attached adhesive halfpenny stamp. Demand grew rapidly, and in 1895 a new size of postcard was permitted called the court card, but there was little room for illustration. In 1899, a year after Frith's death, a new card measuring 5.5 x 3.5 inches became the standard format, but it was not until 1902 that the divided back came into being, so that the address and message could be on one face and a full-size illustration on the other. Frith & Co were in the vanguard of postcard development: Frith's sons Eustace and Cyril continued their father's monumental task, expanding the number of views offered to the public and recording more and more places in Britain, as the coasts and countryside were opened up to mass travel.

Francis Frith had died in 1898 at his villa in Cannes, his great project still growing. The archive he created continued in business for another seventy years. By 1970 it contained over a third of a million pictures showing 7,000 British towns and villages.

FRANCIS FRITH'S LEGACY

Frith's legacy to us today is of immense significance and value, for the magnificent archive of evocative photographs he created provides a unique record of change in the cities, towns and villages throughout Britain over a century and more. Frith and his fellow studio photographers revisited locations many times down the years to update their views, compiling for us an enthralling and colourful pageant of British life and character.

We are fortunate that Frith was dedicated to recording the minutiae of everyday life. For it is this sheer wealth of visual data, the painstaking chronicle of changes in dress, transport, street layouts, buildings, housing, engineering and landscape that captivates us so much today. His remarkable images offer us a powerful link with the past and with the lives of our ancestors.

THE VALUE OF THE ARCHIVE TODAY

Computers have now made it possible for Frith's many thousands of images to be accessed almost instantly. Frith's images are increasingly used as visual resources, by social historians, by researchers into genealogy and ancestry, by architects and town planners, and by teachers involved in local history projects.

In addition, the archive offers every one of us an opportunity to examine the places where we and our families have lived and worked down the years. Highly successful in Frith's own era, the archive is now, a century and more on, entering a new phase of popularity. Historians consider the Francis Frith Collection to be of prime national importance. It is the only archive of its kind remaining in private ownership. Francis Frith's archive is now housed in an historic timber barn in the beautiful village of Teffont in Wiltshire. Its founder would not recognize the archive office as it is today. In place of the many thousands of dusty boxes containing glass plate negatives and an all-pervading odour of photographic chemicals, there are now ranks of computer screens. He would be amazed to watch his images travelling round the world at unimaginable speeds through internet lines.

The archive's future is both bright and exciting. Francis Frith, with his unshakeable belief in making photographs available to the greatest number of people, would undoubtedly approve of what is being done today with his lifetime's work. His photographs depicting our shared past are now bringing pleasure and enlightenment to millions around the world a century and more after his death.

OAKHAM
AN INTRODUCTION

OAKHAM is the county town of England's smallest traditional county, Rutland. Uppingham is the second town, and the villages included in this book are all within 8 miles of Oakham. Mostly, they are large villages like Langham, Cottesmore, Empingham and South Luffenham. Two are much smaller and located just on the border in Leicestershire - Burton Lazars and Little Dalby.

Rutland nearly disappeared into Leicestershire in the 1960s, but was saved by valiant efforts. Some money left over from the 'Fight for Rutland Fund' was used to improve and plant the castle grounds in 1968. However, in 1974 wholesale local government reform could not be successfully resisted, and so Rutland became a district of Leicestershire. But local patriotism remained as strong as ever, even though Rutland was mainly populated by commuters, and after 23 years of agitation plus

OAKHAM, *School House 1927* 80286

10

government re-thinking in several county areas, Rutland returned as a unitary authority. Now we call Rutland a county again, even though its correct title is Rutland County Council District Council!

The return to independence was greeted in April 1997 with a special BBC Songs of Praise and celebrations in all parts of the county. However, because the population of Rutland is only about 36,000, the price to pay for independence has been high: Rutland has one of the highest Council Tax payments in the country.

At the same time as Rutland was fighting for independence, 3% of its valuable agricultural land was flooded to produce England's largest reservoir, Rutland Water, opened in 1976. Universal resistance, with slogans like 'Don't flood Rutland', 'We shall be a towpath round a lake', and 'Rutland, Lake District of the Midlands', early on gave way, as the reservoir landscape matured, to general appreciation of a wonderful recreational facility which has enhanced the landscape and changed lives.

For centuries Oakham was a small town in a small county. In 1801 its population was only 1600. This did not double until 1881. Then the population remained steady at about 3500, even declining in the 1930s. It still did not rise in the 1940s and 1950s, but in the late 1960s the influence of commuters was beginning, coupled with the increase in new housing estates. By 1971 the population was 6,400, and thirty years later it has almost doubled. There is now some danger that this historic market town may outgrow its charm and attractiveness.

Between 1801 and 1991 the population of the county also doubled owing to its convenient location near the A1, London and the south-east, with Leicester, Peterborough and Nottingham all within 30 miles. This has sent property values sky-high as the delights of England's 'Secret County' and Rutland Water become better known.

Yet, despite its small size, Oakham has always been an important centre of trade, administra-

SOUTH LUFFENHAM, *c1955* S486001

tion and justice. From the 11th century the town was divided into Lordshold, based on the castle, and Deanshold, based on the church. The former was held by the Lord of the Manor, the latter by the Dean and Chapter of Westminster Abbey.

The castle was the location for local courts and the Assizes, but in recent years this function has been eroded; Crown Courts may never again be held there, and Magistrates' Courts may be moved to the County Council offices. The Butter Cross and market tolls are still under the jurisdiction of the Lord of the Manor, Mr Jos Hanbury, formerly of Burley-on-the-Hill. There are two busy markets each week, but the renowned cattle market has gone.

Oakham has been the home of several well-known personalities, ranging from the infamous Titus Oates (1649-1705), 'the biggest liar in Christendom', to Sir Jeffrey Hudson (1619-82), 'the shortest knight in history'. Both were born in Oakham. Titus, 'the King of Liars', was an instigator of the Popish Plot (1678).

Macaulay in his 'History of England' described him as having 'a short neck, legs uneven like those of a badger, with low forehead as that of a baboon. He had purple cheeks and a monstrous length of chin'.

Sir Jeffrey Hudson, known as the Rutland Dwarf, was only 18 inches tall from the ages of eight to thirty. Later he grew to 3 feet 6 inches. When he was nine he was taken up to the Duke of Buckingham's mansion at Burley-on-the-Hill on the occasion of the visit of King Charles I and Queen Henrietta Maria; as a dinner-time diversion, he jumped out of a cold pie dressed in a tiny suit of armour. So impressed was the Queen that she took Jeffrey into her service, where he had many adventures.

Lord Lonsdale (1857-1944), the 'Yellow Earl', was the first President of the AA, which adopted his yellow livery. He instituted the Lonsdale Belt in boxing, and was himself a superb horseman and athlete. In 1878 he walked 100 miles from Knightsbridge Barracks to Ram Jam Inn,

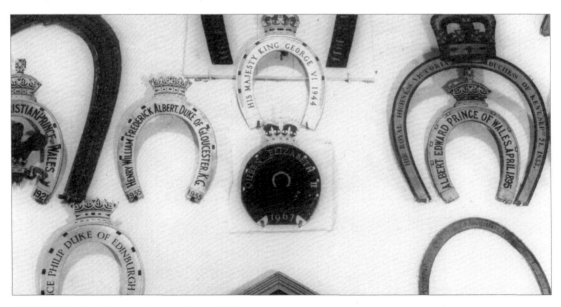

OAKHAM, *The Queen's Horseshoe c1967* O2065

Rutland, to win a wager: he did it in 17 hours 21 minutes. He was Chief Steward of the Jockey Club. His Barleythorpe Stud was famous, and he made one of the biggest jumps, 32 feet, in the history of fox-hunting.

George Finch, 9th Earl of Winchilsea (1752-1826) was the founder of the MCC. His servant, Thomas Lord, acquired the cricket ground at Marylebone, which ever since has been called Lords. Some of the earliest test matches were played in Rutland at his home, Burley-on-the-Hill.

The photographs in this selection are from 1927 to 1965. Apparently, though Francis Frith began his epic photographic survey in 1860, there is nothing in the archive for this area until 1927. In several ways this is advantageous: it is the period within living memory for many people; it had austerity as its theme, from the Depression of the 1920s and 30s to the post war shortages of the 1950s. As the photographs will show, this period saw the rise of the motor car. Additionally, this was the last settled period before the revolutionary changes of the 'swinging 60s'.

The archive is patchy in this area. Oakham is well-served. There is quite good coverage of Uppingham, but many Rutland villages are not recorded at all. The photographers seemed to concentrate on churches, schools, buildings and streets - rather passive features - rather than people, events or activities, and indeed people are scarce in most photographs. However, much can be gleaned by comparison of scenes at different dates, and by observing shop signs and what may be on display outside. As many of the dates of the photographs are approximate, the reader may be able to zoom in on the actual date by any personal local knowledge they may have. We are fortunate in Oakham, because a local printing firm produced 'Matkin's Oakham Almanack' between 1881-1941, which gives residences and businesses street by street, along with many valuable advertisements and other

BURTON LAZARS, *The Church c1955* B890057

town data. Readers in the area can consult the Almanacks in Rutland County Library in Oakham or Rutland County Museum.

Was Oakham ever a rural idyll? Certainly it was a classic English market town, and despite changes it still retains a similar ethos - although the red revolution of brick and Welsh slate has changed its appearance in the last 100 years. Uppingham has avoided the worst of this, and still looks like a stone town.

Arthur Mee described Oakham as 'small with wide streets and fair gardens with trees shading old houses with peeps of green hills and woods and lanes, and wooded paths running to the Market Place'. Did others agree?

The Ellingworth family were well-known in Oakham; they were music dealers and photographers and ran a chemist's shop. Dulcie Ellingworth, one of the daughters, taught at Langham Village School; she lived to a great age, being alive throughout most of the 20th century. When interviewed by A R Traylen in the 1970s, she gave a very evocative picture of the old Oakham. 'We crossed and re-crossed the road to each other's homes to our hearts content, not having to fear traffic, save for a few horses'. The sounds of the day were 'the song of the birds, the rhythm of the anvil at the blacksmith's shop next door and the Angelus'. She said there was never a need to lock the doors, and spoke of the pageantry when the judge came for the Assizes at the castle. The May Fair, the Flower Show, Feast Day and the Horse Show were all very important celebrations. The opening up of the big houses or hunting boxes for the hunting season was a time of great activity and evening entertainments; after this, Oakham 'settled down to its summer siesta'.

This is the world we have lost, and it has gone forever. Frith's photographs, however, capture

LANGHAM, *Cold Overton Road c1955* L337003

something of the time for us to observe, cherish and remember. Oddly enough, the period of these photographs, 1927-65, though stable and still part of the old order, contained the beginning of the end of that order. As we survey the photographic record, we will see that it was in this period that so many landmarks were lost - one side of the old market was demolished for the new GPO; Catmose Street and Bargate earlier in 1914 - the narrow entrances to the High Street - were widened and the frontage in Northgate breached.

'Look thy last on all things lovely' might be our maxim, and Frith's photographs help us to do that for an age that has gone. Today, planners regulate our townscape, they enhance the Market Place and devise schemes to conserve all that is best. Therefore, we should no longer lose precious heritage nor have to fight to preserve it. We hope the planners are doing that for us.

But 'nothing can bring back the hour of splendour in the grass, of glory in the flower'. The Oakham of Dulcie Ellingworth, with its innocent simplicity and calm beauty, has gone forever. But we have Frith's photographs to recall it for us. The Oakham of today has a totally different society with different aspirations, complicated by a dependence on materialism. Yet it has its own special community spirit, and in 70 or 100 years' time maybe future townsfolk will look back on this time with as much nostalgia as we feel when we see Frith's Oakham. Known as 'the Cathedral of Rutland', All Saints' Oakham has a county-wide function, with civic services and ceremonials like the RAF Freedom of Oakham service. Besides, it has a large benefice including 7 other churches.

Queen Edith, wife of Edward the Confessor, had been granted the Manor of Rutland including Oakham and its church. On her death in

UPPINGHAM, *c1965* U10075

15

1075, the king ordered the tithes and advowson of the church to go to the Dean and Chapter of Westminster Abbey, who also held the Manor of Deanshold. This link to the great abbey lasted until the 19th century.

Oakham, its church and hall were mentioned in the Domesday Book (1086). Queen Edith had ploughland, there was a priest and a church - the priest's name was Albert the Clerk. There were 138 villagers and 19 smallholders. As yet, no trace of this church has been found, but it is known that there have been at least three churches on this site; the present church is the most outstanding, and it symbolises 1000 years of historical continuity. Simon Jenkins in 'England's Thousand Best Churches' writes: 'The church tower is magnificent. Rutland steeples are often too thick-set to soar, but not Oakham's'. Rising to 162 feet, the 14th-century steeple dominates the town and is crowned with Cock Peter, one of the oldest weathercocks in the country.

There was a clock on the tower as early as the 17th century, but the present clocks (1858) are notable because the maker, Frederick Dent of London, was involved in making Big Ben at the same time. Hence the Oakham clocks are based on this, and have the Westminster chimes.

The mighty peal of 8 bells has sounded all over the town for all manner of local and national events. On 7 November 1805 the bellringers were paid £1 1s 0d for Nelson's victory at Trafalgar. On 21 June 1813 they were paid £1 1s 0d for Wellington's victory over the French at Vitoria, and on 26 June 1830 they received 3s 0d for the passing and funeral bell for George

IV. Bells were rung for the Millennium and the Queen's Golden Jubilee, as well as many other recent national events.

Inside, the church is supremely elegant, with slender pillars, lofty nave arcades, plenty of light and superbly carved capitals telling the story of the Fall of Man and his Redemption. The famous carving of Reynard the fox shows him with a goose in his jaws, followed by goslings. Nearby is a monkey with a great weight attached to its collar. A man with a broom sweeps the place clean. The popular interpretation of these carvings is that the fox is the Abbey of Westminster taking the Great Tithes, the goslings are the local people, and the monkey is the priest unable to do much about it. The abbot is making a clean sweep of everything!

Religion and education have long been connected throughout history. In Oakham this is physically apparent. The C of E School stood opposite the church from 1855 to 1955, and north of the church in the churchyard lies the Old School of 1584 (restored in 1723), founded by Archdeacon Robert Johnson (who also founded Uppingham School in 1584). Today, Oakham School is a leading co-educational public school with over 1000 pupils. The Old School's walls were decorated with frescoes in 1904 representing the story of Gareth from Morte d'Arthur, executed by Mrs Florence, sister of the headmaster at the time. In 1969 the Old School was developed as the Shakespeare Centre, but it was later restored to its original state.

CHURCH
AND SCHOOL

OAKHAM
From Cold Overton Hill c1955 O2042

Oakham is situated in the Vale of Catmose. The church dominates the view, and the town is arranged compactly around it. In the far distance is a ridge, the site of the mansion of Burley-on-the-Hill. In the far distance rich farmland has now been replaced by Rutland Water, coming twenty years after this photo. Cold Overton road still looks like a country lane. On the left is Corah's factory, and on the right the housing has not yet spread into the neighbouring fields.

▼ **OAKHAM,** *Cold Overton Road c1955* O2034

On the way into town we pass the West End Post Office near the telephone box. Opposite is Pinewood, a large house once owned by the Turner family, later a Nurses' Home (the Rutland Memorial Hospital is further along on the right). The continuous kerb and the shadow of buildings in the left corner suggest that Long Row has not yet been linked in as a road. This would mean that the photo may be earlier than 1955.

► **OAKHAM,** *High Street c1955* O2024

The Regent Cinema opened in 1940, changing its name to the County in 1943. At that time it was Rutland's only cinema. In the early 1950s it was used on several occasions for Oakham School's Speech Day. The film showing at the time of the photograph was 'Silver City' ('Albuquerque' in the USA), released in 1947. The cinema was sold for redevelopment in 1988, and shops and offices now occupy the site. The British Legion Club is to the left of Pink & Jones's van. Further down on the right, the garage was built in 1918 by Dale & Pearce, and later run by Victor Wood.

◄ **OAKHAM**
High Street c1965
O2074

Marshall's the ironmongers is on the left, then Neville House. A little further along is Glaziers, the old-established draper, milliner, outfitter and clothier. At the corner is the TSB, and opposite is Westmoreland's, the electrical shop with televisions and radios. The garage on the right is built on the site of the old town gaol. Beyond is the Memorial Institute, and next door A J Cragg, once a saddlers.

▶ **OAKHAM**
A Thatched Cottage 1927 80288

This charming thatched cottage belonged to the butcher, Mr Buttress. His shop is just round the corner - we can see the awning. A gas light stands on the corner, and All Saints' church rises beyond the trees. Later the cottage was demolished, to be replaced by an ironmonger; TSB moved into the premises in 1964.

19

▶ **OAKHAM**
All Saints' Church and the War Memorial 1927 80289

The church is dedicated to All Saints and the Blessed Virgin Mary. The south porch is the oldest part. A great deal of re-building took place in the 14th century, when many splendid Perpendicular windows were inserted. The tower and spire were completed at this time, but in about 1428, Roger Flore, four times Speaker of the House of Commons, left money in his will to heighten 'Okeham Stepil'. The churchyard was closed as a burial ground in 1860, and the gravestones were levelled and covered over or removed, except for the three shown in the photograph. The war memorial was dedicated in 1922.

◀ **OAKHAM**
The Church, the Nave 1927 80290

We are looking east to the High Altar and the Decorated east window. The restoration of 1857-58 swept away box pews and a gallery, which were replaced by the pews we see. The font is one of the oldest items in the church. It was here in 1619 that Jeffrey Hudson, the famous Rutland dwarf, was baptised. Note the organ of 1872 in the Lady Chapel to the right. The profusion of flowers suggests a Flower Festival. The famous carving of Reynard the fox is on the capital to the right.

▲ **OAKHAM,** *The Church, the Interior 1927* 80291

This view looks into the Trinity Chapel, with the tomb of a wool merchant on the right. On the left, a curtain covers the north door. The same radiators are in use to-day. Looking diagonally right, there is a good view of the organ pipes in the Lady Chapel, beyond the chancel. Note the intricate carving on the capitals.

◄ **OAKHAM**
The School and Church Street c1955 O2036

This view looks from the church tower towards Church Street. The square building on the corner is Garner's the ironmongers - TSB took over Garner's building in 1964. The thatched shop is Strickland's the baker. The Roebuck Inn is nearer the church, and next door is Fords, cabinet makers and upholsterers, the predecessor of the large departmental store of today. The large building stretching across from the left is the old vicarage, later College House, part of Oakham School. Recent discoveries show it to be the oldest house in Oakham.

OAKHAM
The School Sanatorium and Gardens 1927 80287

The 16th-century vicarage, later known as College House, with its beautiful grounds, was acquired by the Trustees of Oakham School in 1880 and 'converted into an admirable sanatorium'. We can see the school chapel to the right and All Saints' in the background. Later, the garden was replaced by a lawn, and in 1972 the Round House for boarders, was built there.

OAKHAM, *The Church 1927* 80295

This view is from Cutt's Close, looking south to the Old School of 1584 and beyond to the magnificent tower and spire of All Saints'. To the left we can see the earthworks of the castle, and below the moat or fishpond. The path across Cutt's Close looks quite neglected.

OAKHAM
*Cutt's Close Avenue
1932* 85152

This is the main public park in Oakham. Originally it was the outer bailey of the 12th-century castle, surrounded by large earthworks. This photograph shows a lovely avenue of limes along the earthworks next to Church Street. There are swings and seats in the park to the left.

OAKHAM, *The Old School and Cutt's Close c1955* O2021

We are looking north from the church tower, with Burley Road to the top right. By this time the park had been developed with a bandstand, a shelter, swings, see-saw and a paddling pool. There are now several made-up paths and many seats. The Old School has an inscription round the outside wall: 'SCHOLA LATINA GRÆCA HEBRAICA A°1584'.

OAKHAM, *The School Chapel c1955* O2035

This view is from the church tower. The gate in the wall opposite the church gate was not there in the 1927 photograph. The school chapel was designed by Mr G E S Streatfield and built by Messrs Bowman of Stamford. It is in the shape of a Latin cross, with short transepts and a short chancel ending in an apse.

OAKHAM
The War Memorial
1927 80297

This is situated in the churchyard to the south of the church. The design was by Mr (later Sir) Ninian Comper, who also designed two altars and a window in the church. The cost was about £1,000. The names of 102 men who died in the Great War are inscribed on it. Oakham School Chapel is beyond the wall. It was completed in 1925 and dedicated in 1929.

OAKHAM, *The School Memorial Chapel 1927* 80292

This is the fine entrance to the chapel. The sculptures represent the common sacrifice and suffering of the nation. They are the work of Mr F W Sargant, the sculptor brother of a former headmaster. The school sanatorium is on the left, with the lovely gardens in front.

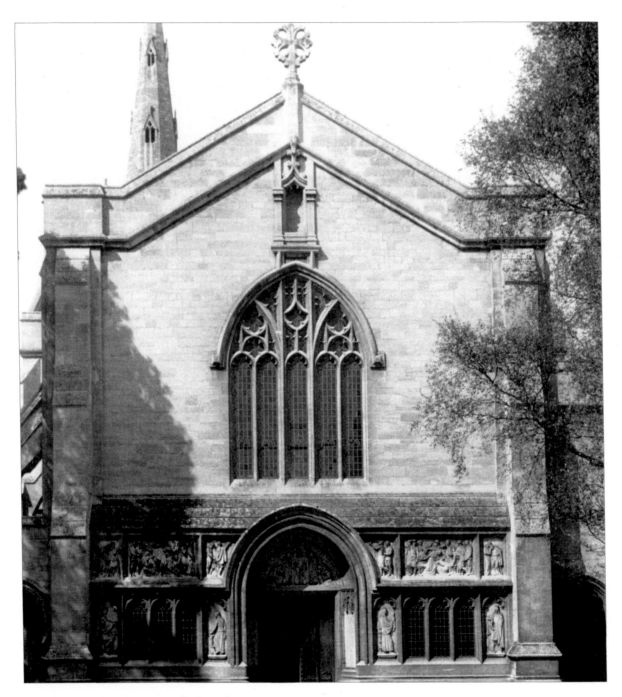

OAKHAM, *School Memorial Chapel c1960* O2051

This later view shows that the gardens have been replaced by lawns and a central pathway; this leads to the 1939-45 War Memorial Library, opened by HRH Duke of Gloucester in 1955. Cock Peter and the church steeple are behind.

OAKHAM
The School Memorial Chapel, the Interior 1927 80298

This view looks from the narthex at the entrance, where there is a gallery for the choir and an organ - but note the grand piano (right). A new organ was installed near the right transept in 1993. At each side of the entrance inside are panels with the names of boys and masters who died in the War. This austere interior once held most of the school, but now, with over 1000 boys and girls, it cannot do so. An alms-dish and silver candle sticks studded with jewels were presented by the relatives of the fallen, to whom the whole chapel is a fitting memorial.

OAKHAM, *College House c1960* O2057

Once the Old Vicarage, then the School Sanatorium, this had become College House by 1965. The fine original doorway betrays its ecclesiastical origins. In 1971 co-education was introduced, and College House became a girls' boarding house. In 1984 it became a Seventh Form Study Centre.

OAKHAM
The Town Centre
c1950 O2037

This view from the church tower looks towards Church Passage and the Market Place. The roof of the Butter Cross is visible. To the right is School House. To the left, the waste ground is where cottages have been demolished to make way for the new GPO, built in 1954.

OAKHAM, *The Old Butter Cross 1927* 80281

The Butter Cross is shown on the town plan of John Speed c1611. Behind, the cottages are part of Oakham School. The gateway leads into Chapel Close, and the School House is on the left.

OAKHAM, *School House 1927* 80286

School House stands at the corner of Market Place and Market Street. The Hospital of Christ, built in 1398, stood on this site, which was once known as Baresplace. School House was erected in 1853. This is the main entrance, with the school crest above the door. Shortly after this photograph, in 1928, music rooms, a library and more classrooms were added to the rear.

MARKET AND CASTLE

The church, Old School, market place and castle are all close together. In fact, if we draw a rectangle bounded by the High Street, Burley Road, Station Road and Church Street they are all located in it. One explanation of this is that Oakham was once a fortified Saxon town, and subsequently development was within these boundaries.

Oakham may have been a Mercian royal centre with a timber hall and associated buildings within this rectangle. By Domesday, this may have become a motte and bailey castle. Then, not long after, William the Conqueror granted the part of his Lordshold containing the church to Westminster Abbey, and this became the separate Deanshold.

In 1166 Wakelin de Ferrers was granted Oakham, and between 1180-90 he built the fortified manor house which we see to-day. It was not a recognisable castle as such, but one of the finest examples of Norman domestic architecture in the country. It had surrounding walls and a moat defining the inner and outer bailey. It is the earliest aisled hall of stone in Britain to have survived virtually complete.

It was a centre of activity, and it is not surprising that the market was close by under its protection. The town grew up around the two. Over the centuries the market has remained more or less the same in its layout. In fact, there seem to be two markets, one off the High Street and the other round the Butter Cross. Could there have been a church market (in Deanshold) and a lord's market (in Lordshold)? Eventually, the focus of the town slipped away from the castle and became centred on the Market, the High Street and even Dean's Lane and Northgate.

OAKHAM, *The Butter Cross and the Stocks 1927* 80280

The Butter Cross is over 400 years old - it is shown on Speed's town plan of c1611. It has a sun dial above the roof with its gnomon. Why the stocks have 5 holes is still a mystery. The cobble floor is loose, just as it is today. F F Budworth, the cabinet-maker and upholsterer, is the shop to the left; next are Glaziers, Miss Payne the optician, and F W Hart the grocer. Near the gas light is J E Smith, tobacconist and stationer.

OAKHAM, *All Saints' Church and Butter Cross c1950* O2018

This exquisite view remains one of the best in Oakham. In the foreground the railings around School House, taken away for the war effort, have not yet been replaced. The Butter Cross is in front of the cottages, and Church Passage leads to All Saints' with its magnificent spire. Behind the tree, houses and shops have been demolished to make way for the new GPO, built in 1954. The large house has supporting beams.

▶ **OAKHAM**
The Old Pump and the Butter Cross 1927 80279

School House is behind the pump. Until 1880 the area in the foreground was a covered market shambles. There are milk churns on the cart, perhaps being delivered to F W Hart, 'Family Grocer, Tea and Provision Merchant'. Note the errand boy's bike propped up against the gas lamp. There is a motor bike and sidecar up near Church Passage; in 1926 a motor cycle combination was bought for Oakham Police - could this be it?

◀ **OAKHAM**
The Old Butter Cross and the Church 1927 80277

A better view of the motor bike and sidecar. Note the window shutter behind. A notice on the Butter Cross warns that no cars are allowed inside. The well-known shop Glaziers (right), 'Draper, Milliner, Outfitter and Clothier', has 'Boys Suits from 7s 11d, Gents Mackintoshes from 5s 11d, Trilby Hats 3s 11d', and as the shop window shows, a galaxy of other goods.

▲ **OAKHAM,** *The Butter Cross 1927* 80278

It is a quiet day, but some repairs seem to be taking place to the left. The row of shops can be more easily seen in this photograph. Miss Payne, Qualified Optician (right), occupies a shop in a large but rather dilapidated building which has a hoist on the side, suggesting that this was a warehouse at one time.

◄ **OAKHAM**
Chapel Close and Butter Cross c1955
O2050

We can see the school chapel beyond the open gates to the left of the Butter Cross. This area, including the row of cottages, was known as Chapel Close. The new GPO, built in 1954, is on the right.

OAKHAM
Market Place 1932
85151C

This excellent view has Castle Lane to the right, with J E Smith on the corner selling all manner of goods from Players, Wills Star and Gold Flake, to local view postcards, wooden hoops, newspapers, magazines and toys. Next door, F W Hart the grocer is still in business - note the errand boy's bike outside. Some years later Glaziers and Harts moved into the High Street. Where is the little girl now?

▼ **OAKHAM,** *The Post Office and All Saints' Church c1955* O2047

The shops and houses we saw in earlier photographs were demolished, and for some years the land was derelict. In 1954 the new GPO was built on the site in a neo-Georgian style in Clipsham stone with a Collyweston slate roof. Despite all the best efforts, the flat roof to the left destroyed the skyline.

▶ **OAKHAM**
The Old Pump c1965
O2072

School House main entrance is behind the pump. The surrounding hedge has grown, but the railings have not returned yet; it was some years later before new railings were added. The trees around the pump have been pollarded.

◄ **OAKHAM**
Market Place 1927
80283

What a refreshing scene! There are so few cars that they can park in the middle of the Market Place. The famous George Hotel with its Hole's Newark Ales sign is to the right. Next door with the awnings is Furley & Hassan, 'Drapers, Tailors, Furnishers', who began near the Butter Cross in 1836 and moved to this location in 1863. On the corner (right) is Whitehouse & Son, 'Gun Makers and Sports Outfitters', established in 1851. On the opposite corner L O Illsley, saddler and harness maker, sells 'the Illsley Sponge Rubber Panel to prevent Galling and Sliding, giving extra comfort to horse and rider'. Perkins, General Merchant's shop is at the far end.

► **OAKHAM**
Market Place c1955
O2022

There is a delivery at the George Hotel, with barrels on the pavement. Now there are many vehicles, including five Royal Mail vans and J H Knight's van - the radio and electrical shop at 35 High Street. Illsley's the saddler's is on the left still; next door is E W Davis & Sons, high-class footwear, including 'K' shoes, Lotus, Delta and all kinds of riding boots made to order.

OAKHAM
Market Place c1965
O2075

Much remains the same. There are still plenty of parked cars, and still 'K' shoes and Illsley's at the corner, but Whitehouse & Son have gone from the right corner.

OAKHAM, *The George Hotel c1950* O2007

This historic coaching inn has been a local landmark since the 18th century. Parts of the building may be older. Election results were announced from the front of the inn. The name was changed to the Whipper-Inn Hotel a few years ago.

OAKHAM, *The Castle Entrance 1932* 85150

This lane leads from the Market Place to the castle gates. The buildings on both sides are located over the original moat. Centuries ago there may have been a drawbridge here. The buildings on the left were demolished to make way for the GPO (1954).

OAKHAM, *The Castle Gateway c1950* O2006

This fine gateway is 13th-century in style, but was rebuilt by George Villiers, Duke of Buckingham, who became Lord of the Manor in 1621. It matched similar gateways at his home, Burley-on-the-Hill. The wrought iron gates were added in 1872, replacing wooden doors. Decorative horseshoes and shields on the gates are a reminder that real horseshoes were once nailed to the wooden doors.

OAKHAM, *The Castle c1955* O2029

This view of the castle grounds looks east from the church tower. Friesian cows are grazing; perhaps they belong to Mr E Ball, who owned property to the right in the Market Place. Beyond the cows, the hill is the site of the original castle motte. Beyond that are the houses along Burley Road.

OAKHAM
The Castle 1927
80296

The splendid horse chestnut tree shades the castle. We can see a recent repair to the roof, and also the carvings on the gable ends of a centaur and Samson with a lion. The additional buildings attached to the west end were modified later (see O2029, Page 41).

OAKHAM, *The Church and the Castle 1927* 80294

This classic view of the castle with All Saints' behind is a favourite for all photographers. The east end shows twin doorways, now blocked. The nearby six-light rectangular window may have been inserted in the 16th century; it was blocked up in the early 1900s. The extension to the Castle on the right was added in the 19th century.

OAKHAM
The Ancient Court House c1950 O2003

The castle was the seat of administration and justice, as well as being the manorial centre. The Great Court Leet, Court-Baron, pleas of the forest, inquisitions, assizes, quarter sessions and petty sessions were held here. There was a gaol in the grounds. The first recorded assize in Rutland was held here in 1229.

OAKHAM, *From Cutt's Close 1927* 80293

This view from Cutt's Close looking south shows how close the Old School is to the church; both are next to the castle. The earthwork around the inner bailey of the castle is clear, and so is the moated area or fishponds below. There is little vegetation on the earthwork, but today it is almost totally covered.

► **OAKHAM**
The Castle, The Great Hall 1967 O2063

The Great Hall has a nave and side aisles divided by two arcades each with three massive stone columns, dating between 1180-90. Above the capitals are the carved figures of six musicians playing different instruments. Four musicians are human, the other two an ass and a goat. Sometime in the past their heads were knocked off. The Great Hall has a judge's bench, jury benches, a witness stand and a dock designed to cater for the Assizes and Quarter Sessions. Most astonishing is the display of more than 200 horseshoes presented by peers of the realm and royalty to the Lord of the Manor.

◄ **OAKHAM**
The Queen's Horseshoe
1967 O2065

Queen Elizabeth II paid her
forfeit with the horseshoe
in the centre. Her father's
is above, made on his visit
during World War II. The
Duke of Edinburgh visited
in 1957. As we can see,
the horseshoes became
symbolic and sometimes
very large. Notice that the
Rutland custom is to hang
the horseshoe downwards:
some say the luck runs out
this way, but we say it stops
the Devil nesting in it.

STREETS
AND BUILDINGS

The first known town plan of Oakham was by John Speed in about 1611. This gives a really good idea about our present-day street pattern and how it evolved. In fact, it confirms that there has been little change in the historic centre of Oakham.

The Market Place is still the pivot, and it has two components: the Butter Cross and the area in front of the castle gate. In the latter an island building divided the Market Place, just as it has done for the last 400 years. The castle and Shire Hall are to the north within their enclosure. Nearby is the Free School and the church. The High Street has at least two narrow points: Bargate and the eastern end. For years these persisted. At each end of the High Street several roads radiated in a variety of directions.

Parallel lanes mirror the High Street to the north. Dean's Lane and Northgate are linked by Church Street. Short lanes like Finkey Street and smaller yards run between many streets. South of the High Street another embryonic road is beginning, later known as South Street. Westgate and Gaol Street link this to the High Street.

Speed's plan shows houses, gardens and orchards, and also crosses. There are six of these, mainly at crossroads, except for the Butter Cross; now only the latter remains. Some crosses might have marked medieval town gates or boundaries. The tithe barn is shown in the northern part of town. The town pillory is marked, and so are Gibbet Gate and Malt Mill Street, now Mill Street.

Both Northgate and Dean's Lane were much busier than they are to-day; and one or both may have been the most important road at one time before the High Street took over that function. Both roads accommodated a variety of occupations: pork pie maker, aerated water manufacturer, bill poster, town crier, printer, tent and rope works, letter carrier, ladies seminary, cycle works, coal dealer, confectioner, tailor, decorator, lodging houses, carpenter, baker and grocer. It was between Northgate and Dean's Lane that much of Oakham's population was concentrated, often in small yards and jitties. The streets and buildings shown on Frith's photographs demonstrate the historical continuity of Oakham's town plan - modifications have been few. Of course, it is outside the historic core that major new estates and roads have been added since the 1960s, and this is still going on.

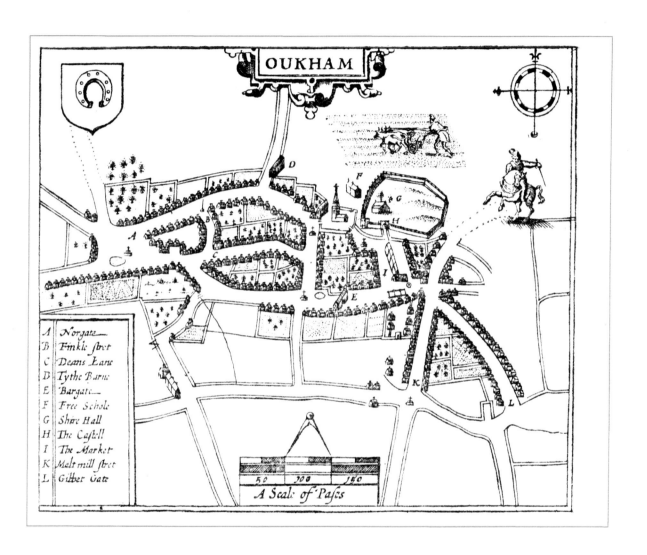

John Speed's Town Plan of Oakham c1611

▼ OAKHAM, *Catmose Street c1955* O2027

This is the very narrow entrance to the High Street from the Uppingham direction. The Bell Inn is on the left. Opposite, Roberts sells stationery, books, toys, fancy goods, art needlework and wools. At the Mill Street corner (right), Smith & Sons the grocer's was taken over by Stricklands. The poster above, 'Your Waste Paper Counts', is a reminder of post-war austerity.

► OAKHAM
Catmose Street c1967
O2073

Here the road has been widened, with parking on the left. The Bell Inn and all buildings on the right have been demolished, and soon a new library will be built. Ahead is another branch of Furley & Hassan. On the left, Roberts is still in business next to George Perrin. At the Mill Street corner, E D Smith Ltd, tobacconists and stationers, once called Bon Marche, is soon to be demolished owing to road alterations.

◀ OAKHAM
High Street 1927
80282

Leaving narrow Catmose Street to enter the spacious High Street and Market Place to the right must have been a surprise to strangers. The old post office is on the left, followed by Matkin's Yard, then Corney's the watchmakers, Barclays Bank, Fowlers the solicitors and the Crown Hotel. In the distance Flore's House juts out. Illsley's and Matkin's the printers are on the right.

▶ OAKHAM
High Street c1955
O2023

The motor car is creeping in, but no parking restrictions can be seen. Basically the street looks the same. On the left is the Crown, Boots (which had moved in recently) and the Midland Bank. On the right, Matkin's corner has a list of town events, and Illsley's window is as full as ever with leather goods. Post Office Telephone vans are still in evidence.

OAKHAM
High Street 1932 85149c

What a patient horse to wait unattended for its master, who is no doubt in the saddler's. It is a delight to see only one innocent car and several bikes. The man crossing the road clearly has no worries about traffic. Beyond is Flore's House and D E Clarke, 'Cash Grocers'. To the left is the stately portico of the Midland Bank.

OAKHAM
High Street 1927 80284

We are looking the other way down the street from Flore's House. On the right is Sharpe Bros, soon to be taken over by F W Hart the grocer moving from the Market Place. Next door is the ubiquitous Furleys, this time wine and spirit merchants; then the Midland Bank, and further along perhaps an ironmongers, with galvanised baths hanging outside. Opposite, in the distance is International Stores - the first sign of the chain store. Coming up on the left side are tea rooms, Housers the watchmaker and jewellers, and Whittle & Son, grocers, next door. It seems that the past is on the left with the horse and traps, and the future on the right. FP1263 is a Rutland number. Registration began in January 1904; George Phillips, Inspector of Weights and Measures, had one of the first cars, an 1898 8hp Decauville, Reg No FP 4.

OAKHAM
High Street c1955
O2025

This is the same view as 80284. F W Hart has moved in on the right. International Stores have moved up on the left, and Furley & Hassan are in their old premises. A B Woodcock, confectioner, is on the left. There are more cars, but still no waiting restrictions visible, and the bicycle is still in the ascendancy.

OAKHAM, *Northgate c1955* O2014

This historic street bends to the left. The sign of the Wheatsheaf Inn is on the left. Opposite is Manor House, perhaps the Manor House of the former Deanshold. We can see the barrier for the school exit on the right.

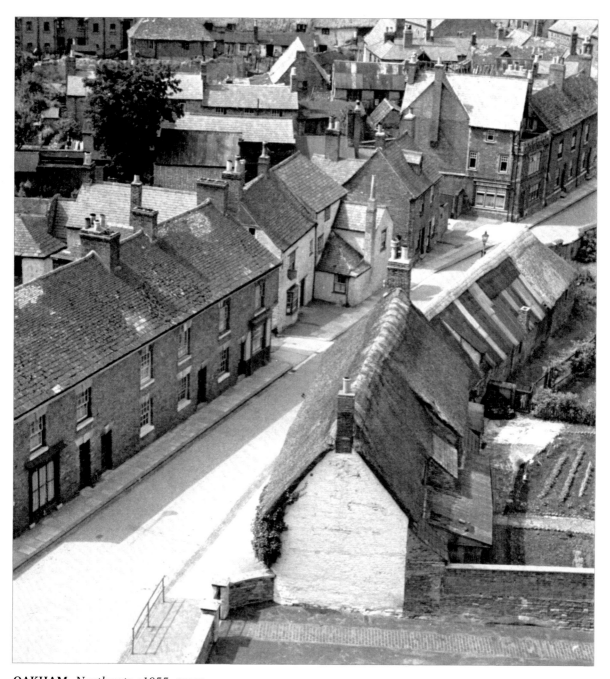

OAKHAM, *Northgate c1955* O2031

This view from the church tower shows part of the C E School playground, with Manor House next to it. Note that some of the cottages in this row appear to be thatched only on the street side. On the left, the Wheatsheaf Inn is just out of shot. After the terraced houses there is a large white house which may be the former Angel Inn, then a private residence. Nearby is Angel Yard; Barlow Road broke through here some years later.

► OAKHAM
Northgate c1955
O2033

Going into Northgate
from the Wheatsheaf,
we see a tobacconist
on the right, then the
entry to Pullin's Yard,
one of the many yards
leading off the street.
Chambers's, motor
and cycle engineers,
are beyond. The large
house on this side of
Chambers's was once
the Britannia Inn, by
this time a private
residence. Beyond, the
cottages are covered in
lovely old wisteria.

◄ OAKHAM
Northgate c1955
O2012

We are looking eastwards
back down the street.
The centre house with
two-storeyed mullion
windows is 16th-century.
Note the excellent thatch.
However, the shop has a
Welsh slate roof, despite
being a stone building.
Perhaps it was originally
thatch, then replaced by
slates, and the dormer
window added.

▲ **OAKHAM,** *Mill Street c1955* O2011

The cottage on the right with the mullioned bay window is reputed to be the birthplace of Titus Oates. St Joseph's RC church stands behind the hedge. It was built in 1883 by the 3rd Earl of Gainsborough, but it closed in 1975. The large stone building next door has been a ladies' school and a maternity home in the past; it is now the Rutland Angler pub.

◄ **OAKHAM**
The Hawthorn Horse 1932 85154

Situated at the corner of Cemetery Road and Station Road, this topiary horse was a local attraction. It was in the paddock of Mr J Littler, a veterinary surgeon. The Old Barn, now Oakham School shop, can be seen to the right.

▶ **OAKHAM**
The Hawthorn Horse c1955 O2045

Apparently the horse remained a feature for some years, until building on this land swept it away. The Old Barn is opposite the row of terraced cottages. To the left is Kilburn Yard. From 1818-78 this was the prison, large enough to accommodate 96 prisoners, but it was little used; later it became stables. Now it has been adapted by Oakham School as the Art and Design Centre.

◀ **OAKHAM**
The County Offices c1955 O2019

Catmose House was a hunting lodge of the Noel family. In 1936 it became the offices of the County Council, having changed hands for £2,600. Since 1880 there have been many changes to the building. Opposite were the Urban District Council Offices and the indoor riding school for the Rutland Fencibles, a volunteer cavalry regiment raised by the Noels in 1794.

▲ **OAKHAM,** *The Church of England School c1955* O2030

This remarkable building, viewed from the church tower, was opened in 1855 and closed in 1955. It was demolished in the 1960s for a car park. The school garden is at the top of the photograph, and the pathway leads to the Headteacher's house. A new C of E school was opened on Burley Road in 1955.

◄ **OAKHAM**
The Cricket Pavilion
c1950 O2010

Oakham CC have a fine ground at the Lime Kilns Field, Brooke Road, which was extended to county size. The pavilion was built in 1938-39 and it was dedicated to the late J M (Monty) Bradshaw. Vandals burnt down the pavilion in January 2002.

OAKHAM
The Fire Station c1955
O2009

Originally, the fire station was at the southern end of Mill Street, next to the Salvation Army Hall. By 1955 a new station had been built on the corner of Brooke Road and South Street. In recent years this has been considerably modernised. In fact, the newer stations were only round the corner from the original site.

BEYOND OAKHAM

Rutland is only 17 miles across in each direction, and has only two towns and 53 villages. With its lovely rural landscape, it has been called 'a microcosm of England'. Generally, it has heavy clay land in the west, producing rich grassland and woodland. In the east the limestone soils encourage arable farming, and the landscape is much more open. Separating these two regions is the Vale of Catmose, in which Oakham is situated; this is a mixed grass and arable area. Ironstones and marlstones produce the red soils which are so characteristic of Rutland, particularly towards Uppingham, where there are a series of ridges and valleys.

For centuries three aristocratic estates gave stability to life and landscape in Rutland: from Burley-on-the-Hill, the Finch family, Earls of Nottingham; from Exton Park, the Noels, Earls of Gainsborough; from Normanton Park, the Heathcote, Drummond and Willoughby families, later Earls of Ancaster. These three estates occupied the centre of this small county, in a sense protecting it against change, until the break-up of the estates began in the 1920s. Some

would say they kept a feudal lid on the county.

When the influence of these great estates slackened, there was always the 'Hall' in every village to keep the social structure of the old order in place. But by the advent of Frith's photographic survey in 1927, a new world was emerging, and village life was to escape from the grip of the lord of the manor and the vicar. In 1925 the Normanton Park Estate was sold and broken up. Empingham was no longer an estate village. The Burley Estate began to sell in the 1930s, and the Burley mansion was sold and converted to flats and private ownership quite recently. Exton village is no longer under the control of its Catholic lord of the manor. As the photographs show, cars, buses and petrol pumps begin to appear, the sign of an emerging mobile society.

Edward Thring, the great headmaster of Uppingham School, led the way to a new world in education, and the impact of the school on the town began to be felt. 'Uppingham School must surely have a prominent place in the history of Rutland'. When he arrived in 1853, there was a handful of mainly day

COTTESMORE *The Village c1955* C434009

pupils. When he died in 1887, there was a 300-strong boarding school with a national reputation. His 'great educational experiment' made him a leading pioneer in education. The school continued to prosper, and the photographs show that many new buildings were erected as the school expanded. Uppingham and Oakham are both large co-educational establishments, great innovators with a big influence on their towns as the school buildings continue to multiply.Uppingham School, led the way to a new world in education, and the impact of the school on the town began to be felt. 'Uppingham School

must surely have a prominent place in the history of Rutland'. When he arrived in 1853, there was a handful of mainly day pupils. When he died in 1887, there was a 300-strong boarding school with a national reputation. His 'great educational experiment' made him a leading pioneer in education. The school continued to prosper, and the photographs show that many new buildings were erected as the school expanded. Uppingham and Oakham are both large co-educational establishments, great innovators with a big influence on their towns as the school buildings continue to multiply.

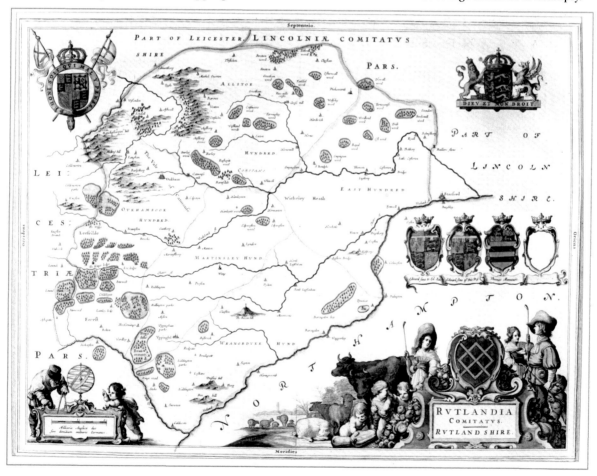

Rutlandshire by J Blaeu 1645

SOUTH LUFFENHAM
General View c1955
S486001

This village, and its twin, North Luffenham, are less than one mile apart in the valley of the River Chater, which originates near Launde Abbey to the west and joins the River Welland at Ketton to the east. Both are historic villages, as their place-names indicate. This view appears to be from Station Road looking south to the church and village. A railway embankment can be seen, probably the Oakham-Stamford line.

SOUTH LUFFENHAM, *The Church c1955* S486004

St Mary's church has a 14th-century 'curiously crocketed spire' (Arthur Mee). Pevsner thinks it is a 'small, fussy crocketed spire'. G E Street restored the church 1852-61. The building to the right may have been a tithe barn. Note that the church is well above river flood levels. In 1794 a gypsy girl, Rose Boswell, was buried in the church, despite objections - a tablet records her story.

SOUTH LUFFENHAM
The Village c1955
S486002

Once this was a water-splash, then a footbridge; now a modern bridge has been installed, with a wider road and footpath on one side. The stone houses beyond cluster close together as the lane goes uphill. This part of the village is separated from the rest by the stream.

SOUTH LUFFENHAM, *The Boot and Shoe c1955* S486005

The inn is well-placed near the busy Stamford Road. Once a coal business, then the village bakehouse and a shoemaker's, it acquired its name from the last occupation - the Boot & Shoe Inn. Opposite was the village spring and pump. Note the thatched roof giving way to tiles. The nearby school sign refers to the New School (1875-1969), by 1972 a private house.

▼ **LANGHAM,** *Cold Overton Road c1955* L337003

This road comes from Cold Overton, a fine Leicestershire village, on the hill just 2 miles away. As the sign shows, in 100 yards the road joins the busy A606 Melton-Oakham Road. This is one good reason for the simple petrol station at the corner - the only one on the whole route - but it is on a nasty double bend.

► **LANGHAM**
Well Street c1955
L337001

Many village lanes had names such as Water Lane, Spring Back Lane, or Well Lane. Usually the pump or spring were nearby. Here it was near the main road in the foreground. Note the steps up to the front doors - there was always a risk of flooding in Langham. The older cottages are down near the church at the far end.

◄ **LANGHAM**
*The School and
School Lane c1955*
L337004

At the Melton sign the A606 does a double-bend. When the village school was built in the 19th century all was quiet, but by 1955 it was getting busier - there are Belisha beacons across School Lane. Can you see the sign of the Noel Arms further down on the left, and the Wheatsheaf on the right? Dulcie Ellingworth was headmistress here.

► **LANGHAM**
*The Church and the
War Memorial c1955*
L337006

SS Peter and Paul's church has a large 13th-century tower with a 14th-century broach spire. Mee thinks 'like no other entrance we have seen is this pinnacled porch' on the south side. Perhaps the splendour of this village church is due to the benefactor, Simon de Langham, born there in 1310 - Chancellor of England, Archbishop of Canterbury and Cardinal.

LANGHAM, *The Church, the Arnhem Plaque c1955* L337008

On 17 September 1944 Sunday morning worshippers on their way to church heard the distant rumble of aircraft engines.
At RAF Cottesmore, a few miles away, the biggest armada of aircraft ever seen in Rutland prepared to move off for Arnhem,
where paratroops were to seize a crossing over the Rhine. They failed with a great loss of life.

LANGHAM
The Church, the Interior c1955
L337007

By tradition, the church is strewn with hay from a field given to the church on the first Sunday after St Peter's Day, 29 June; the custom is associated with the Langham Feast. Note the unusual arrangement of two windows over the chancel arch, and also the faces between the arches of the arcades.

LANGHAM, *The Old Vicarage c1960* L337012

This building is dated 1790, and is a little distance from the church. The church is near the intersection of Well Street and Church Street, and the vicarage lies beyond. The apparent planned layout of the streets in Langham has been attributed to the monks of Westminster Abbey, who owned the village. There is now a modern vicarage elsewhere in the village.

▲ LANGHAM
An Old Cottage and the Chapel c1960 L337011

The church is to the right, overlooking the small Baptist chapel with a small pinnacle on each corner of the front. It has a large graveyard. Nearby is the village hall, built in 1890; it has a plaque outside commemorating the centenary of the Langham Parish Council 1894-1994. The thatched cottage has a very long garden plot, typical of this village.

► LITTLE DALBY
The Church c1955 L32060

This tiny village is 2 miles east of Great Dalby; both lie in the shadow of Burrough Hill (690ft). St James' stands on a hill half a mile away from the village - Arthur Mee called it 'a sentinel on a hill'. Although there are older parts, the tower and much of the rest of the church were re-modelled in 1851-52.

LITTLE DALBY
The Church, the Nave c1955 L32059

The arcades are 13th-century, with a lofty clerestory of the 15th century. There are 12 angels above the arcades. The old stove looks highly inefficient, and a paraffin lamp is suspended on a wire. Mrs Orton, the 'inventor' of Stilton cheese, lived in the village in the 1730s, and must surely have attended this church many times.

BURTON LAZARS, *The Church c1955* B890057

This village is on the A606 less than 2 miles from Melton Mowbray and about 8 from Oakham. A monastic leper hospital was founded here in the 12th century, hence the name, derived from 'Lazarus'. It was the most important leper hospital in England, and closed in 1544. The 13th-century church of St James is a landmark on the main road. The 20ft-high monument is to William Squire, a weaver, who died in 1781. The historian Throsby commented: ' ... a gingerbread tomb ... the baseless fabric of a vision ... upon this partly-coloured pile are urns, arms and leg-bones tied together with a cord, hanging pendant from a jaw-bone ... it abounds with imitations of skulls, angels, crosses and glories'.

▼ **COTTESMORE,** *The Village c1955* C434003

This is the main street, with the Green to the right. In the distance a Bland's bus is manoeuvring - this was the bus company's HQ. St Nicholas's church with its fine 14th-century broach spire dominates the street. Peter Gunning was rector here from 1660 to 1670. He is well-known for the prayer 'For All Sorts and Conditions of Men' which he composed. The inventor of the Rutland plough and the allotment system, Richard Westbrook Baker, is buried in the churchyard, and so is 'Uncle' Edward Chapman Clayton, a famous hunting personality. The village pump was near the thatched cottages on the left.

▶ **COTTESMORE**
The Sun Inn c1955
C434005

The inn overlooks the Green. When RAF Cottesmore opened its base in the 1930s a little distance from the village, many families came to live in the married quarters. Great expansion in the war years and afterwards occurred, and by 1953 there were 3 concrete runways, one extended for jets. This extra population meant that The Sun became the most popular place around

◄ COTTESMORE
The Village c1955
C434009

This is the main street again, with the church gate to the left and Collard's Central Stores on the right - 'Matkin's Almanack' shows a Mr A G Collard to be a grocer in the village in 1939. The tractor and trailer indicate that there are still farms in the village. The Cottesmore Hunt took its name from the village when it was founded by Tom Noel. The hunting fraternity and followers provided a great deal of custom for local shops.

▶ EMPINGHAM
The Church and Church Street c1960 E134014

Empingham is just over halfway between Oakham and Stamford, on the A606. Both Arthur Mee and W G Hoskins eulogised the church, the latter saying that it is 'one of the finest churches even in this notable little county'. In this view from the main road the church is especially dominant. If the photograph had included the Prebendal House just to the right, it would have been even more impressive. Note the petrol pump on the left.

EMPINGHAM
Church Street c1955
E134004

The village shop is on the left, and workmen are repairing the road nearby. St Peter's church is mainly 13th-century, with a tall 14th-century tower and a small but richly ornamented spire and very tall pinnacles. The church was restored in 1894-95, but the splendid exterior was not touched.

EMPINGHAM, *Crocket Lane c1960* E134009

This charming lane near the church has a concentration of thatched cottages. Further along is Jubilee Barn, the original tithe barn of the village. Many houses carry the shield of the Ancaster family, for this was an estate village from the 1760s until 1925, when the Normanton Park Estate of the Earl of Ancaster was sold and dispersed.

EMPINGHAM
Audit Hall Road
c1960 E134007

This is the Oakham to Stamford Road, the A606. Most of the village is to the north-east of this main road. The Regent petrol station was the only one between Oakham and Stamford (except for the single petrol pump round the corner in Church Street). The Audit Hall is nearby, opposite The White Horse. It was used to conduct estate business.

EMPINGHAM, *Main Street and the Methodist Church c1960* E134002

It was this spacious street that encouraged Arthur Mee to describe the village as 'set among fine limes and rich with an avenue of beeches and sycamores'. The church was built in 1890 - previously a cowshed had to serve! On the left is an older house, but the next one looks like infilling of the 1920s/30s.

EMPINGHAM
Post Office Corner
c1955 E134013

This is Loves Lane, which comes off Main Street and goes to Horn Mill. The houses are a mixture, from the prefabricated post-war to the thatched and tiled. The post office is also a savings bank and money order office. There are bus timetables near the little extension, which seems to display shop items - certainly cigarettes are sold. I wonder if Mrs Redshaw is still the proprietor?

EMPINGHAM, *Highfield Close c1960* E134005

At about this time, Rutland villages began to acquire small housing estates, usually on the edges. At first they were council houses, and later private developers came in. As we can see here, the council paid little attention to attractive siting: although Empingham is a lovely village, these houses are just in a monotonous row. However, one concession was that being in a village you deserved a big garden at the back.

UPPINGHAM
From the South
1932 85159

Note the lovely meadow in the foreground. Uppingham itself sits on a ridge, which accounts for the extremely long High Street. SS Peter and Paul's church at the Market Place is on the right, and the turret of Uppingham School Chapel is at the centre. To the left of the chapel there are other school buildings. The large garden belongs to the house in South Street.

UPPINGHAM, *c1965* U10075

In front of the church is the Old School (1584). The Maltster's Arms was the next property on the right, but it was probably closed by 1965. The sign on the left is for The Rose & Crown, officially on Station Road. At one time the cattle market was held on Beast Hill.

UPPINGHAM
The School 1927 80317

There is an uncanny quiet about this scene in High Street West. All the buildings on the right belong to the school. The Victoria Tower, the main entrance, was built by Sir Thomas Jackson in 1894-97. The statue of Archdeacon Robert Johnson, the founder, is in a niche at the front of the tower.

UPPINGHAM
High Street 1927
80318a

This view looks in the opposite direction to 80317. School Lane is on the left next to The White Hart. The large building on the corner is the Great Hall, recently completed by Ernest Newton in 1923-24. Opposite, two gangster-like figures seem uncertain whether to hide or not - after all, they are next to the bank! Further up this deserted street is the Central Private Hotel.

UPPINGHAM, *The School 1927* 80325

This view is from inside the school quadrangle, with the Chapel and School House to the left. In front is the Great Hall, completed only 3 years before the photograph was taken. It has tall transomed windows at the side separated by giant pilasters. Above, the angled turrets and ogee caps give it a distinctive look. Later, the gateway would be moved back level with the Hall.

UPPINGHAM
Market Place and the Church 1932 85156

SS Peter and Paul's church, with its 14th-century tower, big-angled buttresses and tall recessed spire dominates the Market. Queen Victoria's Jubilee Fountain of 1887 is central. On the far right is a hairdresser's and tobacconist's, Stewards. Going left round the corner is the post office, then Hayrs the grocers, and in the Vaults James Thorpe sold Bass and Guinness. In the centre is a hoist. The White Swan is in the corner with Dunlop bicycle shop next door (displaying its wares). The Midland Bank follows, and then a chemist's shop.

UPPINGHAM
Market Place c1955
U10032

The car is starting to rear its ugly head. Otherwise much remains the same. The Dunlop shop is there, but tea-rooms have replaced the White Swan. James Thorpe, wines & spirits is still in evidence, also Hayrs, the grocer. There are toilets on the far right.

UPPINGHAM
High Street c1955 U10013

This is High Street East, looking toward the Market Place. The ogee turret of the School's Great Hall can be seen. There are no waiting restrictions for cars, it seems, but everything is quiet and serene. Boots is on the left - they were here pre-war. On the right is the Crown Hotel; I wonder if Mr W H Clarke was still the landlord? Almost next door is Price & Sons, boot and shoemaker. The High Street was full of interesting and historic houses, many dating back to the 17th century, like the one on the right.

INDEX

FRITH PRODUCTS & SERVICES

Francis Frith would doubtless be pleased to know that the pioneering publishing venture he started in 1860 still continues today. Over a hundred and forty years later, The Francis Frith Collection continues in the same innovative tradition and is now one of the foremost publishers of vintage photographs in the world. Some of the current activities include:

INTERIOR DECORATION

Today Frith's photographs can be seen framed and as giant wall murals in thousands of pubs, restaurants, hotels, banks, retail stores and other public buildings throughout the country. In every case they enhance the unique local atmosphere of the places they depict and provide reminders of gentler days in an increasingly busy and frenetic world.

PRODUCT PROMOTIONS

Frith products are used by many major companies to promote the sales of their own products or to reinforce their own history and heritage. Frith promotions have been used by Hovis bread, Courage beers, Scots Porage Oats, Colman's mustard, Cadbury's foods, Mellow Birds coffee, Dunhill pipe tobacco, Guinness, and Bulmer's Cider.

GENEALOGY AND FAMILY HISTORY

As the interest in family history and roots grows world-wide, more and more people are turning to Frith's photographs of Great Britain for images of the towns, villages and streets where their ancestors lived; and, of course, photographs of the churches and chapels where their ancestors were christened, married and buried are an essential part of every genealogy tree and family album.

FRITH PRODUCTS

All Frith photographs are available Framed or just as Mounted Prints and Posters (size 23 x 16 inches). These may be ordered from the address below. Other products available are - Address Books, Calendars, Jigsaws, Canvas Prints, Postcards and local and prestige books.

THE INTERNET

Already ninety thousand Frith photographs can be viewed and purchased on the internet through the Frith websites and a myriad of partner sites.

For more detailed information on Frith products, look at this site:
www.francisfrith.com

See the complete list of Frith Books at: www.francisfrith.com
This web site is regularly updated with the latest list of publications from The Francis Frith Collection. If you wish to buy books relating to another part of the country that your local bookshop does not stock, you may purchase on-line.

For further information, trade, or author enquiries please contact us at the address below:
The Francis Frith Collection, Unit 6, Oakley Business Park, Wylye Road, Dinton, Wiltshire SP3 5EU.
Tel: +44 (0)1722 716 376 Fax: +44 (0)1722 716 881 Email: sales@francisfrith.co.uk

See Frith products on the internet at www.francisfrith.com

FREE PRINT OF YOUR CHOICE
CHOOSE A PHOTOGRAPH FROM THIS BOOK
+ £3.80 POSTAGE

Mounted Print
Overall size 14 x 11 inches (355 x 280mm)

TO RECEIVE YOUR FREE PRINT

Choose any Frith photograph in this book

Simply complete the Voucher opposite and return it with your remittance for £3.50 (to cover postage and handling) and we will print the photograph of your choice in SEPIA (size 11 x 8 inches) and supply it in a cream mount ready to frame (overall size 14 x 11 inches).

Order additional Mounted Prints
at HALF PRICE - £12.00 each (normally £24.00)

If you would like to order more Frith prints from this book, possibly as gifts for friends and family, you can buy them at half price (with no additional postage costs).

Have your Mounted Prints framed

For an extra £20.00 per print you can have your mounted print(s) framed in an elegant polished wood and gilt moulding, overall size 16 x 13 inches (no additional postage required).

IMPORTANT!

❶ Please note: aerial photographs and photographs with a reference number starting with a "Z" are not Frith photographs and cannot be supplied under this offer.

❷ Offer valid for delivery to one UK address only.

❸ These special prices are only available if you use this form to order. You must use the ORIGINAL VOUCHER on this page (no copies permitted). We can only despatch to one UK address.

❹ This offer cannot be combined with any other offer.

As a customer your name & address will be stored by Frith but not sold or rented to third parties. Your data will be used for the purpose of this promotion only.

Send completed Voucher form to:
The Francis Frith Collection,
19 Kingsmead Business Park, Gillingham,
Dorset SP8 5FB

Voucher for **FREE** and Reduced Price Frith Prints

Please do not photocopy this voucher. Only the original is valid, so please fill it in, cut it out and return it to us with your order.

Picture ref no	Page no	Qty	Mounted @ £12.00	Framed + £20.00	Total Cost £
		1	Free of charge*	£	£
			£12.00	£	£
			£12.00	£	£
			£12.00	£	£
			£12.00	£	£
			£12.00	£	£

Please allow 28 days for delivery.
Offer available to one UK address only

* Post & handling	£3.80
Total Order Cost	£

Title of this book . . . .

I enclose a cheque/postal order for £ . . . .
made payable to 'The Francis Frith Collection'

OR please debit my Mastercard / Visa / Maestro card, details below

Card Number:

Issue No (Maestro only):   Valid from (Maestro):

Card Security Number: Expires:

Signature:

Name Mr/Mrs/Ms . . . .

Address . . . .

. . . .

. . . .

. . . . Postcode . . . .

Daytime Tel No . . . .

Email . . . .

Valid to 31/12/18

Can you help us with information about any of the Frith photographs in this book?

We are gradually compiling an historical record for each of the photographs in the Frith archive. It is always fascinating to find out the names of the people shown in the pictures, as well as insights into the shops, buildings and other features depicted.

If you recognize anyone in the photographs in this book, or if you have information not already included in the author's caption, do let us know. We would love to hear from you, and will try to publish it in future books or articles.

An Invitation from The Francis Frith Collection to Share Your Memories

The 'Share Your Memories' feature of our website allows members of the public to add personal memories relating to the places featured in our photographs, or comment on others already added. Seeing a place from your past can rekindle forgotten or long held memories. Why not visit the website, find photographs of places you know well and add YOUR story for others to read and enjoy? We would love to hear from you!

www.francisfrith.com/memories

Our production team

Frith books are produced by a small dedicated team at offices near Salisbury. Most have worked with the Frith Collection for many years. All have in common one quality: they have a passion for the Frith Collection.

Frith Books and Gifts

We have a wide range of books and gifts available on our website utilising our photographic archive, many of which can be individually personalised.

www.francisfrith.com

Free Print – see overleaf